BLUE
ROBERT BURTON

Newton-le-Willows

Published in the United Kingdom in 2023
by The Knives Forks And Spoons Press,
51 Pipit Avenue,
Newton-le-Willows,
Merseyside,
WA12 9RG.

ISBN 978-1-916590-00-7

Copyright © Robert Burton 2023.

The right of Robert Burton to be identified as the author of this work has been asserted by them in accordance with the Copyrights, Designs and Patents Act of 1988. All rights reserved. No part of this publication may be reproduced, stored in a retrieval system, transmitted in any form or by any means, electronic, photocopying, recording or otherwise, without prior permission of the publisher.

Contents

Empty Space	7
Like a Stone	9
Imago	12
Drunk Dialling	14
Mandragore / Dead Man's Hand	15
Vampire	18
Blue	22
Fly	24
Fly Fly	25
Fly Fly Fly	26
Rick Shapiro	27
Rearview Mirror	28
Bug Killer	29
Aura	30
Script	31
Blue Again	32

BLUE

BLUE

Blue

Empty Space

Told you weakness
told you my
told had weakness
spoke at last and
told
weakness
that I asked every time
every time
where you were from
what made you so
what made you
enough to
stop me like that
like
no-one could
stop me that way

clear my mind
and stop me
they got tired of my
asking
same thing every time
what made you
stop me
like I came just to
see you

maybe hope
stops me that way

the idea I have
you
more a feeling
I can't explain
exact shape
of an empty space

Robert Burton

calls me selfish
said I was shy and had
that weakness
can't speak
said you are
working though it every day
said you were
waking now
working through
silence

said my
country made me
made me silent
gave me quiet
gave me
nothing
gave me
just myself
knowing what
I want
same thing
gave you
that smile
gave me you

Like a Stone

The moment you lean into me
the end of the day
                parting
and are mine entirely
I do nothing
it is a moment I have come to regret
it is a moment
I used to regret

the day you seem like a stone
I
become a second poker face
and wonder what it means

recast it as a lack of tensile strength
a kind of folding
not suitable for construction
unable to withstand other
forces I don't know the
names for

denying any knowledge
of me
my shadow leaves
says on its way
what hurts is
doubt

I say this too but only to myself
I might shrug it off
shooter wins
sounding like a good sport to
hide corrosion
questions that eat when I don't

Robert Burton

but I'm not a good sport
in the dark layers are
falling away and hidden
without a scent to let you find
the fruit I can peel with one hand
I've lost it too

the mirror tells me
that I have no reflection now
vampire or ghost

scared of my double
I move away
         sidestep
                 skip rope
slip into alleys
and shed my skin
becoming something else
if a voice breaks the evening
I don't hear my call or yours

becoming my doubt I
detach my shadow
and let it leave with the gold
of being me
while I'm scared of your judgement
and take new forms

your hair brushes across my
face
clear that it's quite intentional
I don't move and ask why

in a dream
my reflection
my shadow form a triangle with me
as a corner

taking aim
and see who will be the first to blink
sometimes all we want is to know
where the gold is
sometimes all we need is a drink of water

judgement
passes round the shooters
in second guesses
no one draws and
it comes to rest with you

as
I take its shape
you become my reflection
and close up
the moment has passed

Robert Burton

Imago

It is spring I
burst through my
skin with a second skin my
back stares imago
splits imaginal
watching my self on film
there is a moment
when I don't know which one I am
where the second skin works
beneath the living outer skin

mirrored
everything doubles
before it bursts
becomes
brittle emptiness
crushed skeletal
between a kid's thumb and finger

two skins for
a single moment
before it cracks
a seed shell
second screen
there is an image of
everything
my eye sees
there
has seen
heavy branch
of winter
shadow of the spring
for a moment
nothing is lost

the
sky tastes colour
has sound and a shape

Blue

crushing my shed skin
wonders
is it my body and I am dead
or the skin a snake drops
with anything it no longer needs

for a moment I have
a true image

there is fresh air
season change
and there is rain
where my new body is still soft
and grows wings

spring
leaves on green wet wings
as ghost or echo
a soft clean body
starts
leaves work behind

some light
gets through the rain
people I love? friends
dropped
before take off
everything blurs

not
knowing whether I'm
here or the shell
have I
left myself
empty
separated from truth

Robert Burton

Drunk Dialling

It is
4 maybe 5 am
I can't
sleep and want
to see your face
more than anything
I try to touch your
image just to see that
picture bigger
and hit call
an accident of course
I cancel before you pick up
later you ask
if I am with friends again
have drunk too much
that's it
      I say
            take the out and
pretend you're right
that I'm hot blooded and
senses are altered
swallowing anything real
it sounds better that way
better than
I'm sober
and want you only
because I'm the same
or that I didn't
mean to call

Mandragore / Dead Man's Hand

Take me away
ends a curse
hold a candle
creating sleepers
I can enter the house
but no-one is there
flame
still too cold
to warm or dry clothes
hurt breaks again
you are gone and I am too
saying nothing
to stop anything early at all

heaven baby a
prayer is lost
sky play
ground still is cold
approaching us all unchanged

star born bad tidings
bring
tear in eye
ask
heal love
ask again
not enough
end road

end
word nowhere
page is blank
never done
things
are not there

Robert Burton

dream night
bar chair
corner
glasses so fake
going to sit and buy
a drink for anyone there
just something to dull whatever
is felt at this time

neon is lonely
showing the way as lost
telling there's a
free room upstairs
purple script offers
end
frustration offers
soundtrack pickup
so much is
promised

angel shine
your best boy
is a
promise
you make me these
gold words
they become solid when they
touch air the
spell of your voice
has broken like
grey morning
where I realise I don't know you at all
spent time imagining you
were someone lost to me

morning
casts doubt on gender
or just doubt
has to attach somewhere
nonintentional like desire

doesn't know another way to turn
making everyone into whatever
shape returns me to you

I'm still there waiting in your old room
my old room with
light voice now in the right place
wrong time the
message of love
gets old
but I don't
returning to point
of commencing
so that you too return to that place

only the time is wrong

Robert Burton

Vampire

i

My skin is so good you say
agreed
and you can hear me
shout it from the next room
you too should use sun cream
even on cloudy days and right through
winter freezes
as I say it there is a roll of
thunder and soft rain
takes another five years away
like the heavens are keeping
me young for something
I won't tell my secret
and you don't really understand
but there are things I still
have to do and I will stay like this
until I do those things
at that moment I will crumble
probably to dust
a shower of golden particles
lit by a ray from the sun
as it passes through an open curtain
if there is sun at just the right angle
and just the right time and someone
to see it
and if someone has opened the curtain
otherwise just gone

ii

Dark sky
empty winter
I realise
there's nothing
I need
and laugh
you lose your power
and disappear
a beautiful storm

I never iron
and wear a jumper over
my shirt
I haven't showered
and don't really care

Robert Burton

iii

The stone in my hand
I start to become its colour
my skin like a giant's
stone skin
that a hero has slept
covering his
own body so he can't
move
my forehead is stone
completely

I try to speak and
lift my
body
lift a giant's leg
with my little finger
throwing the stone
away with my hand
but I can't

the stone resembles the words
I can't say
dumb
absence given weight and
a shape

and suddenly quick
a second arthropod hand
rears many jointed out
its stone my skin
hangs two legs
in the dark
after rain
cradles and runs
a body that
holds
my mouth and

feeds me stone
sedatives
sews my nylon mouth
shut

I become its hardness
and do nothing
cold tongue in a blind head

I would
block that carnivore hand
with my hand
if I were
quick and strong enough
to say anything at all

I try to move again but I can't
my forehead petrified into
questions is a
stone forest
        brother doubt

my anger
still can't decide
if the second hand is
mine
that fills my mouth and
disappears there
so it hangs around
doesn't know how to forget

wants to fight the choke hand
that has become a friend
when it returns
waiting to see it run
from the light I will turn on
when it comes and I reach first

Robert Burton

Blue

As a boy I wanted to
invent dreams
and drew my machine
it made everything one
colour and that was how it
started
the colour was blue and
when everything was blue a
user could begin to dream
blue was a colour
was a temperature and a sound
blue was a feeling and a film
a mood
you are born to
about a creator where I
saw the star on a poster
offering one night only previews
and had to go just to see her
and revive a memory of you
because her colour and your
colour were beautiful
and are what the blue becomes as it
deepens
and a taste of
coolness and calmness
removes heat
turning to the pillow's other side
taking away the beginnings
of a stress headache or
a trapped nerve that never
fully develops just hangs
the way a close sky promises
thunder gives only discomfort
and a little sweat and shortness
of breath and the nausea of
a half communicated message

it was also the taste of a drink
coolest and freshest water
from far away and an altitude
where people are lost
never just a name or the
colour it became radioactive and glowing
at any time of day so unnatural
dropping through the sky of that colour
the artist's blue its
infinite depth
capturing a coast
and its weather
not talking or acting
knowing exactly
to breathe without
any dirt that stains your organs
the colour of your shirt
unworried
judgement drops away a weight
unconcerned what others think
in that colour there's focus
not caring if this is the sound of a cassette
or a note on a mirror the
floating conflation of day images
making new forms possible
and anything at all
the beginning of sleep
it was not the heat of my anger
or anyone else's

Robert Burton

Fly

Fever started

    black fly mouth inside my shin

saw it resting its body
    black legs
      mouth's cutting parts needle
              through seven layers

    scissor mouth shuffles strata

          a brush through
          pipe burrows

young strange fluid in clockwork labella

        blood folds
        in dirt eggs

     becomes device
         metal bug
           the glow
           of foreveries

black wings
    body
      head
       swallowed by my wound

  the start of disease

and I become the fly's mind I stopped and too wet to sleep I only can wonder which is which whose blood is whose now the same fly that turned in a painter's mind spreading its eggs on the soft tissue of his mouth's inside in the fever of his dream now enters my dream like a second coin in an arcade slot here comes a new challenger

Fly Fly

Regret crushing it the way
I had right into me it felt so good
even if there were so many other ways
taking something back
it brought violence I
smashed like a god
said yeah
drawing out that syllable
now I started to swim in
green water
olive
      grey
            night water
dirt of a Baltic sea
didn't heal blood
turning my mind to sweat
churning and
breaking in
snakes from a story where the
sea is cursed and becalmed
one wave is another and
the sound of a witch's voice
promises of things I
never wanted
making me need those things
right now
makes me turn in my sheets
just one more time
crawls
enough to make my heat break cold
revenge
revivified lives in my mind
sits behind my eyes
gives me a sore neck
delivers a promise

Robert Burton

Fly Fly Fly

Lifting
my dream
sickness a
silver ball falls planar
sleep its
surface 6.5 degrees
fever takes me
puts me in a '90s
pin: Bram Stoker's Dracula
metallic
storyline into the drain

on the playfield my fever rolls and hears
xenon words
I have crossed
oceans of time
racking up points
dot matrix graphic blood red rare variation
much is to be learned from the
ways of beasts I have crushed into my leg
the count has a special message just for me
Attila's blood is in his veins no witch or devil
so great as the fly's blood in mine
it seems
I'm already Nosferatu
a dinosaur screams
wanderer
commands a revenant
rise from the grave and
rescue my daughter
out of sleep we have all
come mad
all night one thing becomes another
Tom Waits grins and eats flies

Rick Shapiro

Asked me had I ever
needing it so much
just for the money
and if I had would I feel bad now
wake up sucking my thumb in the foetal position
wanting ice cream
calls me
Neo Nazi techno boy
uptight
a kind of contradiction
like the guy with a crew cut
talking about left hooks and the Dodgers
a real asshole
knowing nothing of life
told me later it was all part of the act
of course it was
best thing I've ever done

Robert Burton

Rearview Mirror

On the ground your tears are red gold
falling to the sea they turn amber
trapping your sorrow
with your love forever
solid and smooth and hard
and beautiful
just as it always was and can't change now
after these years you still search
take disguises for your journey
change names and meet new people
show them absence how character
shapes a road skateaway
another city
tell them keep walking
no one can stop until
you've burned right down
worried there's a little cigarette smoke in
your hair and a line no-one else can hear
you look later and they're gone
changed
before you and before you
notice
the feeling has lost its heat
subalternate
satellite decreases
shifts in the rear view is clearer
than before compressed as it
falls away
pared heart
apple pajamas
cool moon is silver
approached and
swallowed is white
leaves your sky empty
disappears

Bug Killer

Surrounded by the
aura of a saint
the blue light
of a bug killer
may they be drawn
and you do
nothing
watching beneath water
as in slow motion
they explain they know
everything
understand
what you want
not to take your money
around a street corner
only to
leave promising
somewhere warm
and alone
a nice dream

Robert Burton

Aura

Another way of pretending
say
you don't know how

your disciples
beg for answers
you explain
if it's going to happen then it will
and can't be stopped
or ended

if it doesn't
don't care
it's kind of the secret
to just wait and see

but they don't get it
are confused
say too much
and are entirely transparent
the way jokes aren't funny
if you have to explain

you smile and
go back to acting
mixing
truths with lies
give nothing

you tell them you just have to
endure tension
but they can't
uncertainty isn't their thing

searching for answers hear them say
what you say or do hardly matters
you're so handsome and leave
part right

Script

You play
falling into their plan
so comfortably
guess things you know already
index finger
touching one of your lips
and you have to play like this
like it isn't getting old
just to step over bored

Robert Burton

Blue Again

The touch of your mouth
without effort as it has to be
I scatter in the greatest joy
borrow someone's web of stars
someone no-one
there is no you
and I go
anywhere again
everything is painted blue
free and cool the colour descends
behind my eyes
a low light
washes out the day
is calm says
how long have I waited
sleep and the
sons of sleep
deceptive of all things
take your shape
a tree and branches
bring you home
with straight black hair
hand on your waist
icicle moon tells
how long have I waited
its face so cool runs a
silver tear
aerial aerofoil
bends whatever light is there
lifts
reflects the start of
my dream
I can finally sleep
the shape of your mouth
without effort breathes
sea swell
frost of
borrowed stars

www.ingramcontent.com/pod-product-compliance
Lightning Source LLC
Chambersburg PA
CBHW011958060426
42444CB00046B/3461